MY ANIMAL KINGDOM

D0240607

ELEPHANTS

Brown Watson
ENGLAND

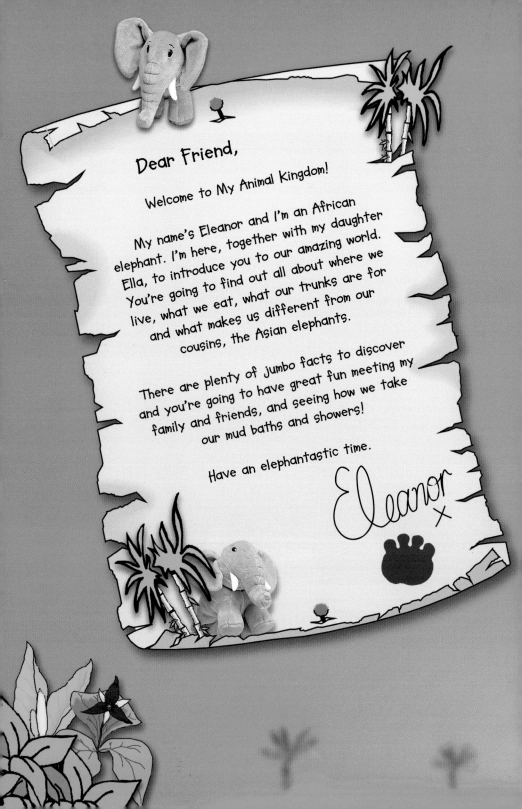

Dear Friend,

Welcome to My Animal Kingdom!

My name's Eleanor and I'm an African elephant. I'm here, together with my daughter Ella, to introduce you to our amazing world. You're going to find out all about where we live, what we eat, what our trunks are for and what makes us different from our cousins, the Asian elephants.

There are plenty of jumbo facts to discover and you're going to have great fun meeting my family and friends, and seeing how we take our mud baths and showers!

Have an elephantastic time.

Eleanor
x

CONTENTS

Let's look inside!

4

LOOK AT ME

Elephants are huge! They're the biggest land animals alive today. A male elephant, called a bull, can be more than three metres high – that's about the height of two people standing on top of each other! Because they are so big, elephants need a lot of food. They spend most of the day munching plants and grasses.

I can flap my large ears to keep me cool.

I use my trunk for eating, drinking, smelling, touching and showering!

My long tusks are great for tearing bark from trees and digging up tasty roots.

I need strong, muscular legs to carry me – I'm a real heavyweight!

4

ELEFACTS

LATIN NAME: *Loxodonta africana*

ANIMAL GROUP: mammal

ANIMAL FAMILY: Elephantidae

COLOUR: grey/brown

SIZE: Adult male elephants can be up to 4 m tall. Females are smaller, measuring up to 2.5 m. A fully grown adult male is about 7 m long – not including its trunk and tail!

TUSK LENGTH: up to 3 m

WEIGHT: up to 6.5 tonnes!

SPEED: reaches 40 km/h, but normally ambles along at 4–6 km/h which is the same speed as people walk

EATS: grass, roots, bark, shoots, leaves and fruit

DRINKS: water – about two bathfuls a day!

LIVES: 60–70 years

Well, I never knew that!

My wrinkly skin helps to protect me from the sun. It's also tough, so I don't get scratched by rough trees and bushes.

I have four flat toes on my back feet and three on my front ones.

DID YOU KNOW?

TIP-TOES

● Elephants actually walk on tip-toe, like a ballet dancer! Their toes are spread flat on the ground and take most of their weight. By tip-toeing along, they can walk very quietly.

● An elephant's feet are large, round and flat to support its enormous weight.

● Having flat feet helps elephants to wade through mud without sinking.

Elephants have big heads, long trunks and huge ears. They also have the largest brain of any living creature – four times bigger than a human brain! They have good eyesight but sound, touch and smell are more important to them. An elephant's trunk is a very special piece of equipment. It's a nose, a top lip and a hand all in one. The elephant uses it to touch, hold and smell things. It is delicate enough to pick up a pea and strong enough to tear branches from trees.

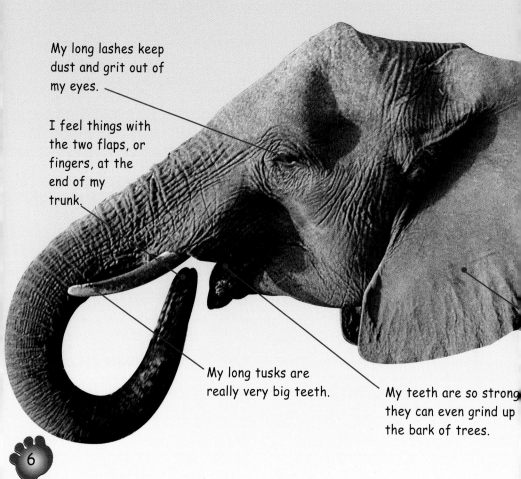

My long lashes keep dust and grit out of my eyes.

I feel things with the two flaps, or fingers, at the end of my trunk.

My long tusks are really very big teeth.

My teeth are so strong they can even grind up the bark of trees.

TOOTHY!

African elephants have two types of teeth. Their tusks are really incisors – teeth used for tearing. They also have massive molars for munching.
The molars get worn down fast, then new ones, growing behind them, push the old ones out.

Adult elephants have two tusks made of ivory

Molars, which get replaced up to five times in an elephant's life

HEAD TO HEAD

There are two main types of elephant: the African elephant and the Asian elephant. At first they may look very similar but there are several differences to watch out for.

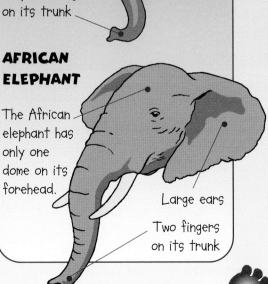

The Asian elephant has two bumps, or domes, on its forehead.

Smaller ears

Only one finger on its trunk

ASIAN ELEPHANT

AFRICAN ELEPHANT

The African elephant has only one dome on its forehead.

Large ears

Two fingers on its trunk

My ears are big and wide. With my excellent hearing, I listen for other elephants when they trumpet, blow, puff or rumble to me.

African elephants live in most parts of Africa except the desert. They live mainly on the savannah or in the bushlands. A savannah is a wide grassy plain. It is very, very hot and there isn't much shade. Bushland is like the savannah except that there are more trees and bushes and the land may not be quite so flat. Some African elephants live at the edges of forests where it is a little cooler, but most prefer to roam the savannah.

> I need a sunhat!

DID YOU KNOW?

- The African elephant is more dangerous than its Asian cousin, and is more likely to attack people.
- Asian elephants live mainly in forests, not on open plains.
- People have been training the gentler Asian elephant for hundreds of years.

WHERE IN THE WORLD?

Asian elephants live in parts of India and South-east Asia. But there are fewer elephants in the world now. This is because they have had to make way for people. When people build houses and cities get bigger, the elephants' natural habitat – their home in the wild – is destroyed. People also kill elephants for their ivory tusks.

AFRICAN ELEPHANT

ASIAN ELEPHANT

EUROPE

This is where we all live.

ASIA

AFRICA

INDIA

AUSTRALIA

African elephants share the plains with lots of other animals. They sometimes help these animals by accident! Elephants are very messy eaters – they tear down branches and scatter leafy scraps which other, smaller plant-eaters can eat. But too many elephants in a small area is bad news. Elephants need to eat so much that they sometimes tear down trees faster than new trees can grow.

He's very big, Mum!

RIVER HORSE

The hippopotamus is a very big animal. Its name means river horse. It does not compete with the elephant for food or for land. The hippo spends most of its time in rivers and lakes. It likes to swim along and graze on water plants.

HOW ARE ELEPHANTS HELPFUL?

BIRDS

Birds, such as cattle egrets, snap up the insects which elephants disturb as they walk through the long grass.

CREEPY-CRAWLIES

Thousands of beetles, flies, worms and other creepy-crawlies love to feed on elephant dung!

PEOPLE

People often follow elephant pathways through the forest. The elephants have trampled these paths so much that they are really easy to see.

PLANTS

Many seeds pass whole through an elephant's stomach. Then they grow in the elephant's dung!

KEEP CLEAR

Leopards are meat-eaters, but they are not big enough to attack elephants. Even lions, which are bigger than leopards, won't attack an elephant. Some of the other animals that live on the savannah, like the African buffalo in the picture below, are very fierce and will charge at most animals, but even they keep well clear of elephants.

Elephants live together in large groups or herds. Everyone is related – mums, aunts, sons, daughters and cousins. There are about 20 elephants in a family group. Adult males, called bulls, usually live alone or in bachelor groups. They still need to stay near their herds so that they can fight off other bull elephants. Young elephants are called calves. A female calf often stays with her mother and helps to look after her brothers and sisters. When young male elephants are old enough, they are chased away from the herd by their father.

Uncle Edward enjoying a long, cool drink.

Young Ella was two months old when this picture was taken.

Eric and Ernie practise fighting.

Me, baby Ella, Auntie Ethel and Ernest on a day out in the bush. We had a lovely trip and are now on our way back to the water-hole.

Baby elephants don't need to find their own food – their mothers go on feeding them for several years. This means that the babies have lots of time for playing. But their games are really a way of getting ready for adult life. Young bulls play-fight with each other, practising for the future when they will have to fight other males to protect themselves and their herd. Young female elephants help their mothers to look after even younger members of the herd.

I was born in July!

LEADING LADY

There is always one female elephant in charge of each herd. She is called the matriarch and is usually one of the oldest females. She is experienced and wise, and decides where it is safe for the herd to eat and drink.

BABY FILE

BIRTH

Female elephants, called cows, sometimes give birth to twins. But usually they have just a single calf. Other females often help the newborn calf and its mother. They also protect the baby from any unfriendly neighbours. Less than an hour after it is born, the baby can stand up.

UP TO FOUR YEARS

Baby elephants have lots to learn. Mum and the other elephants all help them though, pulling the calves out if they get stuck in the mud and protecting them from danger. It takes about four months and lots of practice for a baby to learn how to use its trunk. Baby elephants drink their mother's milk until they are about four years old.

OVER FIVE YEARS OLD

This is when young bulls leave the herd.

BIG FEET

The world must seem like a forest of huge grey legs to a baby elephant. It has to learn not to get under everyone's feet!

KEEPING COOL

Staying cool in the African sun isn't easy for an animal as big as an elephant. That doesn't mean it can't be fun, though. Like people, when elephants are really hot, they take a shower. Elephants are especially lucky because they can use their trunks as hose-pipes to squirt water over themselves or each other. It takes a bit of practice, but with good trunk control an elephant can squirt water all over its body!

Watch where you're flicking that mud, Eric!

THE COLOUR OF MUD

Elephants spend so much time rolling in mud and having dust showers to cool them down that the colour of their skin actually depends on the colour of the local mud! Red, black and even yellow elephants have been spotted coming away from a good mud bath.

MUD, GLORIOUS MUD!

A favourite way of beating the heat is to have a mud bath! Elephants love to plaster themselves with gooey mud. The mud is cool and refreshing. When it dries, it also helps to protect their skin from the fierce sun.

DID YOU KNOW?

FANTASTIC FANS!

An elephant's ears provide another clever way of staying cool. Elephants can use their ears as fans by flapping them backwards and forwards to make a cooling breeze. And their big ears also have lots of tiny blood vessels in them. By flapping their ears, elephants cool the blood in these vessels. The cool blood is then carried to the rest of the body to keep their temperature down.

DUST OFF!

Unless you're lucky enough to find a big tree, there's not much shade on the savannah. So, to help stop their skin from burning, elephants cover their backs with dust. The dust also helps to keep the biting insects away.

WHAT I EAT

Elephants have big appetites. An elephant can eat up to 200 kg of food a day – which means its daily food weighs as much as the total weight of three adult people! It's no wonder elephants spend up to 18 hours a day munching. They eat mainly grass, but leaves, twigs, bark and fruit are also on the menu. During the dry season, when the grass dries up, they have to eat more from trees and bushes. To find enough food, a herd needs a large area to roam in.

SALTY TASTE

All animals need salt. Plant-eaters don't get any from their normal diet, so they look for it in the soil. Places with especially salty soil or rock are called salt licks. These Asian elephants are enjoying a good, salty lick!

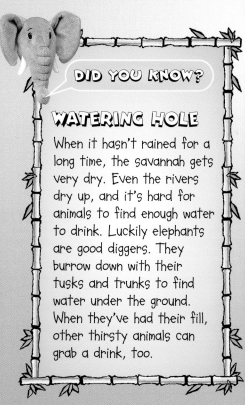

DID YOU KNOW?

WATERING HOLE

When it hasn't rained for a long time, the savannah gets very dry. Even the rivers dry up, and it's hard for animals to find enough water to drink. Luckily elephants are good diggers. They burrow down with their tusks and trunks to find water under the ground. When they've had their fill, other thirsty animals can grab a drink, too.

ON THE MENU

Foraging for food takes up a big part of an elephant's life. Elephants who live near forests may not have as much grass to eat as their savannah friends, but there are lots and lots of different plants to choose from in the forest.

TREE-TOP TREATS!

Trunks are very useful for reaching tasty tree-tops! Elephants can stretch their trunks up to pick yummy fruit and berries. Bananas are a favourite treat.

Elephants are so big that they have no animal enemies. Life can be tough on the savannah, though. Like other animals, elephants are in danger from starvation and drought during the dry season. They can become sick or injured, too. An injured elephant may not be able to move to find food and water. The other elephants will always look after it, helping it to stand and supporting it.

DID YOU KNOW?

When an elephant dies, the other members of the herd may bury the body – covering it with branches, grass and earth. If they see an elephant skeleton, the herd may sniff the remains, remove the tusks and scatter the bones. They may also pause at the place where a relative has died – perhaps remembering it.

Don't leave me behind!

IVORY HUNTERS

Elephant tusks are made of a hard, creamy—white substance called ivory. People once carved it into ornaments and jewellery. Thousands of elephants were hunted and killed for their tusks. In most African countries, hunting for ivory is now banned. But illegal hunters, called poachers, still kill elephants so that they can sell the tusks.

THIRSTY WORK!

Elephants sometimes need to go on long, hard treks to find enough food and water for the entire herd.

5:00 AM It's still dark, but we elephants don't sleep much – we're too busy eating. I've managed to snatch a few 20-minute naps.

6:00 AM Sunrise, and other animals are waking up. I just keep on eating. It's the wet season, so there's plenty of grass.

8:00 AM Little Ella has been practising her trunk control with my tail! Baby elephants spend most of the day playing but they have things to learn, too.

10:00 AM Very hot, so we headed for a water-hole. It's time for a nice long drink and a cooling dip.

12 NOON Emma, my best friend, and I decided it was too hot, so we plastered on some mud and settled down for a nap. Ella likes the shade, so she stretched out in my shadow.

3:00 PM Hungry again, so Auntie Ethel, our matriarch, led us in search of more food.

4:00 PM We bumped into another herd. I haven't seen Edwina for ages, so it was good to catch up on the news.

5:00 PM Saw some humans – they pointed those funny boxes at us and made them click. We stayed away from them – humans are noisy and can be dangerous.

Sunset and back to the water-hole. The babies practised squirting water over their backs! They ended up wetting us all! Ella's dad, Edgar, was there.

It's dark, but that doesn't matter to us elephants – we usually find our food by smell and touch anyway.

I found a fantastic tree, perfect for a good rub. It feels great to scratch off all that caked-on mud and all those irritating little insects.

Cool at last! It's the best time of day for eating. Everyone was happily munching away. Sometimes someone reaches out a trunk, just to say hello.

After eating, it's time to sleep. It won't be long before the day starts again and I'll wake up hungry!

Eleanor x

23

The African elephant and the Asian elephant are the only two kinds of elephant alive today – but there are two groups of animals which are related to elephants, even though they don't look a bit like them. The first group is the hyraxes – little furry animals that look a bit like rabbits – which also live in Africa. Hyraxes may be much smaller than elephants but they can be just as noisy! The second group looks a bit like seals and lives in the water – they are called dugongs and manatees.

WOOLLY MAMMOTHS

The woolly mammoth was related to the elephant and looked very similar. It is extinct now, which means there are no mammoths alive today. They lived in cold parts of the world over 40,000 years ago. They were larger than elephants, had long, shaggy hair to keep them warm, and tusks up to 5 m long – longer than a car!

BIG NOSE!

The elephant seal gets its name because of its huge nose but it's no relation to true elephants at all!

MERMAID MYSTERY

Dugongs and manatees, distant relatives of the elephant, are strange-looking creatures which live in the water. Some people believe that stories of mermaids began when sailors saw dugongs in the water. They thought the dugongs were mermaids – a cross between people and fish!

DID YOU KNOW?

Animals that have a long or big nose are often given names with the word elephant in them. The elephant shrew is actually tiny but it has a long, pointed nose! There is even an elephant-snout fish!

MAN AND ME

Everyone loves elephants because they are so big and strong, and also because they seem gentle and wise. In some parts of the world, people even worship them as gods. In India, there is a god called Ganesha who has the head of an elephant. Other people believe that touching an elephant can help you see what is right and wrong. For special occasions, people in parts of Asia decorate elephants with jewels and paint them with bright colours.

That looks like hard work!

WORKING ELEPHANTS

In Asia, people train elephants to push and carry logs. Elephants can carry small logs in their trunks but they push larger ones along. People sometimes ride on elephants to journey from place to place. Elephants are also trained to perform for people in circuses and zoos. All these things can sometimes be cruel.

ELEPHANTS AT WAR

In the past, elephants were used in war. They were dressed up in heavy armour and soldiers rode them into battle. They would have been a scary sight for a soldier travelling on foot! Over 2,000 years ago a famous soldier called Hannibal led 40,000 men and 38 elephants from Carthage in North Africa to attack the Romans in Italy. Men and elephants travelled through Spain and across the French Alps. The elephants may even have crossed the River Rhône on rafts!

WHAT DOES IT MEAN?

EXTINCT
An animal or plant that has died out. If an animal is extinct, it means there are no longer any of its kind left alive.

FORAGING
Searching for food.

HERBIVORE
An animal that eats only plants and no meat. Humans who eat no meat are called vegetarians.

IVORY
A hard creamy-white substance. The tusks of animals such as elephants, walruses and hippopotamuses are made from this. For a long time people carved ornaments from ivory and valued it highly. Some people even believed it had magical properties.